I have nothing to worry
only on what I can contr

MW01288696

I AM enough.

I am committed to accomplishing my goals, despite all the mistakes I make along the way.

I am beautiful and worthy of every truly beautiful thing.

I am in control.

I release my desire to be "perfect."

I know life is too short to dwell on negativity.

The words "I can't" are not in my vocabulary.

I am on the path to greatness

No matter what happens, I give myself credit for daring to try.

I am in control of my life.

I choose to be myself & allow others to be themselves.

I am willing to forgive.

I will recognize my good qualities

I embrace success.

I know that my approval is the only kind that matters.

I am making space for more success to come into my life.

I take my goals seriously.

I embrace this opportunity to be better than I was yesterday.

I release all feelings of jealousy.

I choose to honor my desires today and always.

I trust myself to make good decisions.

I don't have to wait until I feel "ready" to take action on my goals.

I embrace the infinite possibility of today.

Fear flows through me but it is not me.

That reason does not include gossip & negativity

Fear does not define me.

By forgiving others, I set myself free from pain &
suffering.

I choose to focus on being positive and productive.

I don't need the approval of others because I approve of myself.

I refuse to let anything or anyone hold me back

I am committed to my own success.

I'm meant to do BIG things.

Instead of being discouraged by how far I still have left to go, I choose to be grateful for how far I've already come.

I choose to walk the bright path to my own happiness.

I surround myself with love and light.

I release my need to compare myself to others.

I am good enough.

I know that I was put on earth for a purpose.

As soon as I commit to my ideal life, the universe will start moving on my behalf.

I will not let anyone "make" me angry today.

I go out of my way to meet people I admire & respect.

I am brave enough to embrace my true power.

I can achieve whatever I want. I can have what I desire.

I honor my life by doing what I love.

I release my attachment to everything that no longer serves me.

I am in charge of my own happiness.

I am free of believing that my options are limited.

I am ready to show the world who I am and what I have to offer.

I am ENOUGH just as I am.

I am right where I need to be.

I will plant only GOOD seeds in the world today.

I am responsible for my emotions and reactions.

I don't have to compete with anyone for anything.

Everything is possible.

I choose to radiate love, joy & gratitude today.

I release all feelings of envy.

I don't need anyone's approval before I make a decision.

Forgiveness is a gift I give myself.

I accept responsibility for my own happiness.

I trust my inner wisdom and intuition.

I am comfortable asking for what I want because I know I deserve it

I am bigger than fear.

I honor my desire to reach my goals.

I give myself permission to walk MY path.

I choose to forgive.

I am the only one who knows what's best for me.

I am focused on doing what I was put here on earth to do.

I refuse to believe my own excuses.

I let go of my excuses.

I don't need anyone or anything to complete me because I am already complete.

I will allow myself to evolve

I embrace my full potential, even if it makes others uncomfortable.

Forgiving myself and others releases me from the pain of the past.

By doing at least ONE thing everyday, I make consistent progress toward my dreams.

Nothing stands between me and my highest good.

I choose to be at peace.

I let go of the belief that I need someone to "make" me happy.

I forgive and I am free.

I have enough.

My life is free from drama and negativity.

I am committed to finding at least one hour of "me" time today

I am not lacking in any way.

There is nothing wrong with me.

I am enthusiastic about life & ready to take
inspired action on my goals.

I choose to do what's best for ME.

Even if I take a wrong turn, I can find another route.

I know that I have nothing to prove.

I judge myself by my own standards of success.

I refuse to allow myself to be overcommitted.

No one can make me angry.

I say NO quickly and easily.

I take responsibility for my choices today and always.

My body is celestial

I release all negativity from my life.

I am destined to live my OWN version of happy that has nothing to do with anyone else.

I am allowed to acknowledge all that makes me human

I know I am enough & have enough.

I am productive & focused on results.

I am calm in the face of conflict.

I release my need to impress others.

I take action on my goals now so I can have the lifestyle I want.

I choose to take action in spite of my fear of failure.

I am here for a reason

Instead of complaining about not having ENOUGH time today, I will use the time I DO have in a way that honors my values and goals.

I accept the truth that the past cannot be changed.

I choose to focus on my future and move forward in the light.

I choose to take responsibility for my own happiness.

I deserve to be happy and free.

I give myself permission to SHINE.

I will love myself unconditionally

I have full control over my life.

I am ready to let go of everything that no longer serves me.

I protect my "me time" because I deserve it.

I will not waste even one precious second in anger, hate or jealousy.

I am in the right place at the right time.

I release all negative thoughts.

Regardless of the situations which confront me, I know that I am blessed.

I release my attachment to everything that no longer serves me.

I am thankful for this beautiful day and the infinite possibility it holds.

I am no longer afraid of the unknown because I know I can overcome ANY challenge that comes my way.

I am enough

I allow myself to be open to new opportunities and possibilities.

I maintain a positive mindset despite challenges.

I have choices in all situations.

I know what I want.

I am committed to being a positive influence

Instead of judging others, I judge myself on whether I'm being the best I can be.

I embrace my BEST self today.

I release my need to control the future.

I am deserving of respect

No matter what happens today, I will remember the truth that I am beautiful, powerful and free.

I am worthyI will surround myself with positive people

_____

_____

_____

_____

_____

_____

_____

_____

_____

_____

_____

_____

_____

_____

_____

_____

_____

_____

I know something good is going to happen

I refuse to play small.

I refuse to allow others to hold me back from doing what I really want to do.

I will not conform to the ways of my enemies

I embrace the challenges & opportunities facing me right now.

No one can stop me from fulfilling my purpose

I am not fear.

I am committed to the possibility of my own success.

I am committed to taking action in spite of fear, knowing that all of my needs will be taken care of by the universe.

I am on the right path and I trust myself to make the right decisions.

I brush annoyances off quickly & easily.

I know that my time here on earth is limited.

I am beyond fear.

I agree to disagree.

I choose to let go of the OLD so that I can finally start making progress with the NEW path I want to take in my life.

I choose to live in a way that will bring peace, joy, and happiness to myself and others.

I honor my need to rest and recharge.

I am free to create my OWN reality.

Made in the USA
Monee, IL
20 February 2020